"What a day!"

"Let's test our sleds today!" says Jed.

"I have my big, red sled."

"I have my big, yellow sled," says Jessy.

They will test the sleds at the park.

They go up a little hill.

Zip! Off they go on the sleds.

The sleds are fast! They can go so far.

"That was the best," says Jessy.

Jed and Jessy see a big hill in the park.

"We can test the sleds on that big hill,"

yells Jessy.

Up the big hill they go.

Zip! Down they go.

The sleds are going fast, too fast!

The sleds are going far, too far!

"Stop, stop!" yells Jed. "See the !"

Zip! They just miss the  !

They fall into the snow.

"That was not fun!" Jed tells Jessy.

"Let's go back to the little hill."

"Yes," says Jessy, and off they go!